IT'S TIME TO EAT
APPLE PECAN SALAD

It's Time to Eat APPLE PECAN SALAD

Walter the Educator

Silent King Books
A WhichHead Entertainment Imprint

Copyright © 2024 by Walter the Educator

All rights reserved. No part of this book may be reproduced in any manner whatsoever without written per- mission except in the case of brief quotations embodied in critical articles and reviews.

First Printing, 2024

Disclaimer

This book is a literary work; the story is not about specific persons, locations, situations, and/or circumstances unless mentioned in a historical context. Any resemblance to real persons, locations, situations, and/or circumstances is coincidental. This book is for entertainment and informational purposes only. The author and publisher offer this information without warranties expressed or implied. No matter the grounds, neither the author nor the publisher will be accountable for any losses, injuries, or other damages caused by the reader's use of this book. The use of this book acknowledges an understanding and acceptance of this disclaimer.

It's Time to Eat APPLE PECAN SALAD is a collectible early learning book by Walter the Educator suitable for all ages belonging to Walter the Educator's Time to Eat Book Series. Collect more books at WaltertheEducator.com

USE THE EXTRA SPACE TO TAKE NOTES AND DOCUMENT YOUR MEMORIES

APPLE PECAN SALAD

It's time to eat, come gather near,

It's Time to Eat

Apple Pecan Salad

A tasty treat is waiting here!

Crisp, fresh apples, red and green,

The yummiest snack you've ever seen!

Slice the apples, nice and thin,

Let's get started, let's begin!

Sweet and crunchy, each small bite,

This salad's sure to bring delight.

Add the pecans, brown and round,

A nutty crunch, a happy sound!

Into the bowl, they softly fall,

Apple pecan salad for us all!

Drizzle honey, smooth and sweet,

Or yogurt makes it extra neat.

A little toss, a gentle swirl,

Now it's ready, give it a whirl!

It's Time to Eat

Apple Pecan Salad

Little hands can help create,

This salad's fun to decorate.

Layer colors, red and white,

Eating healthy feels just right!

We sit together, every chair,

Passing bowls with love to share.

Crunch and munch, a perfect treat,

Apple pecan salad can't be beat!

What's your favorite, big or small?

Juicy apples, we love them all!

Green ones tangy, red ones sweet,

Both together are a special feat.

Pecans add their nutty flair,

A little magic here and there.

Each small bite's a joyful song,

It's Time to Eat

Apple Pecan Salad

This salad makes us all feel strong.

The bowl is empty, that's okay,

We'll make more on another day!

Fresh and healthy, bright and fun,

Apple pecan salad's number one!

So next time snack time comes around,

Grab your apples, they're homebound!

Mix and munch, it's pure delight,

It's Time to Eat

Apple Pecan Salad

Apple pecan salad feels just right!

ABOUT THE CREATOR

Walter the Educator is one of the pseudonyms for Walter Anderson. Formally educated in Chemistry, Business, and Education, he is an educator, an author, a diverse entrepreneur, and he is the son of a disabled war veteran. "Walter the Educator" shares his time between educating and creating. He holds interests and owns several creative projects that entertain, enlighten, enhance, and educate, hoping to inspire and motivate you. Follow, find new works, and stay up to date with Walter the Educator™

at WaltertheEducator.com

www.ingramcontent.com/pod-product-compliance
Lightning Source LLC
LaVergne TN
LVHW052010060526
838201LV00059B/3952